HEROES OR TRAITORS:
A SHORT TREATISE

by

Thomas L. Poteet

BOOKS BY TOM POTEET

THE WINDS OF CHANGE

PIECES OF THE PUZZLE

MUSINGS – QUESTIONS & OBSERVATIONS

DEDICATED TO ALL
THE MEN AND WOMEN
WHO SERVE

TABLE OF CONTENTS

PROLOGUE

I was watching the evening news and saw a preview of a forthcoming evening-news special. The preview portrayed one of my favorite evening news anchors speaking with a young man who had stolen secrets from the U.S. government and had given them to a foreign news outlet. The young man was no longer living in the United States. He was being shielded by another nation. In the preview, there was an inference that this young man might be a hero . . . might have done something worthy and heroic in giving away how this nation collects intelligence. I turned it off. I have not been able to watch the evening news on this network since. Whether it was the news anchor's idea or the network's idea to interview this individual doesn't matter to me. The implication that a traitor is a hero is what matters to me.

So my thoughts turned to the following questions:

Who should be considered a hero? What behaviors are we looking for in our fellow citizens?

Why does the government not explain how it develops the offensive and defensive capabilities needed for current and future conflicts with our adversaries? There are no secrets related to how we, as a nation, develop our offensive and defensive capabilities in order to protect and defend our citizens and warfighters. The processes and philosophy are a matter of public record.

Why are we not more concerned, as citizens, with weapons of mass destruction over systems for mass intelligence? Who do we think are watching over all of these offensive and defensive capabilities; or do we think anyone is watching over them at all?

Why do the media make us think the government is listening in on everything we say? Is that even possible?

Is there a better way for an individual, who truly believes they are a patriot, to get the attention they feel they deserve in presenting what they believe is unfair?

I decided to answer each of these questions in the following treatise . . . based on my experience working at the Department of Defense (DoD). My answers are short . . . with the hope that they will spur further conversation. I do not expect all to agree with my answers . . . I am simply attempting to get the conversation started.

I have worked for the DoD for over 30 years in several capacities. I am now retired from the DoD; however, I still work as a consultant to a company that supports the DoD as one of its clients. I spent enough time in the DoD to know that the soldier, the warfighter should always come first in any discussion of defense. They are the individuals who fight our conflicts. They are the individuals who often give their lives so that we can have these conversations.

I spent twenty years of my life working in the chemical and biological research arena for the Department of the Army. I started, in the early 1980's, working on chemical agent weapon deterrents. That is, I worked with a team of professionals to design and produce chemical munitions that would deter the use of similar munitions from other countries. I continued working in the chemical arena until part of my job (twenty years later) was to destroy those same chemical munitions, which were designed as a deterrent. I thought my career, in chemical agent research, had come full circle.

It was then, in my career, that I moved to the National Security Agency (NSA). I spent my final years in government as a civil servant at the NSA. I belonged to the acquisition corps . . . those individuals who support the development of new capability and the improvement to current capability at a defense or intelligence agency. I supported the mission of NSA as do many others. I was never in an operations organization at NSA. I was what they call an enabler. I worked to enable operations by developing and managing contracts and by watching over how contract dollars were being spent.

Watching the news, seeing a young person being praised, seeing a young person unravel much of the efforts and dollars spent on equipping this nation with the best and latest technology to deter our adversaries has brought me to question our current values . . . has brought me to question what behavior we want and expect from our fellow citizens.

It is not my intent, in this treatise, to cast judgment on an individual. I am neither a judge nor jury. It is not my intent to discuss civil liberties with this treatise. My ideas of civil liberties will differ from others. It is simply my intent for others to think about the issues I am about to present and begin a conversation related to the safety of this nation.

HEROES

I'd like to begin my treatise with those I consider to be heroes. My list is long. I find many heroes to exist. I also can identify some superheroes in my lexicon . . . those who go beyond my definition of hero.

I believe that anyone who gets up every day and goes to work to support his or her family is a hero. Anyone who works, pays taxes and pays their way through life performs a heroic duty. Anyone who supports themselves and/or others, with minimal complaints; and with loyalty to their employer I consider heroic. Too many you say. Well, there should be many. If one can work, and they do work; and they support their family; and they support their government; well, I tip my hat to them. They are worthy of my esteem.

Let me give some examples of my definition. I consider my dad to be a hero. My dad was born in 1912. He never got past the 8th grade. He was partially blind in his left eye. He was not allowed to serve in World War II because of his vision. He worked on an assembly line building airplanes instead. He had to borrow $5 to marry mom since the banks had closed because of the great depression. Until he could find permanent employment at the General Motors plant in Baltimore in 1935, he worked odd jobs. There was never a time when he did not work. He found work somewhere so that he could provide a life for him and mom. He worked at the General Motors plant for about 38 years. He also sold real estate in the evenings and on weekends. He also painted cars in his spare time. He was an artist. He was an honorable man. He worked as many jobs as he could to provide for us and so that his three sons could go to college . . . and maybe have it easier than his 8th grade education allowed him. He paid his taxes and he paid his and mom's way through life. He left mom enough money so that she could pay her way and medical expenses for the ten years she remained on this earth after his death. He was and is a hero to me.

I consider my father-in-law to be a hero. He served as a pilot during World War II. He had perfect vision back then. He worked at the Bethlehem Steel Plant at Sparrows Point in Baltimore; then at

Bethlehem Steel's Headquarters in Bethlehem, PA for more than 40 years. He got up every morning and went to work. He provided for his wife and children. He paid his taxes and his way. Bethlehem Steel declared bankruptcy awhile back. Since then, Nan's dad has lived on his Social Security . . . those dues he paid for more than 40 years. At 93, he still pays his bills, gives to his church and volunteers five mornings a week at a local nursing home and hospital. He is a hero to me.

I consider our sons to be heroes. They have all worked since high school. They bought their own cars at an early age and paid for their own car insurance. Since high school, they have been gainfully employed . . . even while in college. They have paid their taxes and have provided, together with their spouses, for their children. We have eleven grandchildren. They are well taken care of. Our children work to provide for their families. I cannot be more proud.

I consider those who serve the public to be heroes. Those who teach our children are heroes to me. Those who serve in the military are heroes. Those who protect and serve through law enforcement and fire protection are heroes.

I would also consider any of these heroes who lay down their lives, for others, to be superheroes. Those who work in the military, law enforcement and fire protection are naturals for my superhero category. More and more, however, I see teachers reaching that same plateau. Because, whenever there is a man-made or natural disaster hitting our schools, I see teachers protecting their students (our children and grandchildren) with their lives. That classifies them, in my book, as superheroes.

I consider most women to be heroes. I have spent 50 years working. I have heard thousands of conversations, from women in the workforce, about stopping on their way home from work and picking up groceries and preparing supper for their family and taking the kids wherever they needed to go after school. When I hear them speak, it is about family. It is not that some men do not do the same. It is just that I have seldom heard those conversations from men. Some of the biggest and toughest men I have had the pleasure to work with still call their moms on a regular basis . . .

sometimes every day. It is their moms who gave them the guidance and values necessary to make it in their careers. It is their moms about whom they speak. I hear about dads and ballgames and cars. It is mostly the moms who have made their value mark on their sons and daughters.

So . . . therefore . . . there are many heroes in this world in my book. These heroes are solid citizens, who work every day, pay their taxes, take care of their loved ones, and provide for themselves and their families. They are heroes to me. I remember my dad, when I was a teenager, driving me through the streets of Baltimore City, by those row homes with the white marble steps, and telling me, preaching to me, that these are the people who have made this country great. I remember as if it were yesterday. My dad's values are mine . . . people who work hard and pay their dues are those who should be the heroes of our lives.

Before I leave the subject of who heroes are to me, I'd like to add that sports figures and celebrities are heroes, to me at least, in line with my previous definition. If they show up for work, when they have work to do, pay taxes, provide for themselves and their families, then they fit my description of a hero. I do not believe they should be idolized. They may have phenomenal talent; but so do many doctors, scientists, engineers, teachers and those who serve and protect. I believe we often look at celebrities as heroes whereas they are simply very talented people, many of whom make a lot of money.

. . .

Then who are not heroes to me? Well, first of all, those who call themselves heroes would not fit my category of hero. I find calling oneself a hero to be similar to calling oneself generous. If you are truly generous, then you don't need to say that you are. If you are truly a hero, you don't need to say it. Others will know . . . that is all that matters. Calling attention to oneself is in no way heroic. Read about and listen to the Medal of Honor winners. They are a humble lot. They are superheroes to me. They have sacrificed their lives for others. They have put others before themselves. They do not refer to themselves as heroes.

15

I would not consider someone a hero who goes to work every day and steals from his or her employer. I'm not talking about walking away with a pen or pencil. I mean stealing money or information from the place where they work. One who steals is either an embezzler or simply a thief. Saying that you're stealing something to help someone else is a lie. You are stealing. You are a thief. And, if what you are stealing includes trade secrets than you are involved in industrial espionage. If you are stealing secrets from the federal government or any government agency for that matter, than you are a traitor. It is that simple to me. And, maybe even worse, if you have pledged your allegiance to a federal agency, representing our country, and you have sworn to uphold their laws, then you betray the agency to whom you swore allegiance, then you are a liar, a thief and a traitor. I do not know how to make that plainer or clearer.

THE CAPABILITY DEVELOPMENT PROCESS

Whether we rely on automobiles, mass transit, houses, commercial buildings or information technology we rely on capabilities that others have designed and built. For example, buses are a mass transit capability that exists because there was an original requirement or need for them to move a bunch of people from point A to point B. Some individual, or most likely a team of individuals, developed the bus capability, which has subsequently morphed into many capabilities. If the bus is moving school children, then it is designed for that capability, which is pretty much a basic capability of mass transit. If the bus is moving people through a city, then it designed for that capability, which may use a different engine with different fuel; or maybe is designed to be a little more comfortable than a school bus because the passengers are paying adults, who have the option of traveling to work or play using a different transportation capability (e.g., a bicycle, motor cycle or personal car). If the bus is moving people for long distances and who are paying a little more to go, then it may be designed to be more comfortable and with rest rooms . . . so that it doesn't have to stop often; and maybe people can take a nap during their journey. If the bus is moving rock stars, then it may be more like an apartment on wheels. So . . . different capabilities follow different requirements . . . even if the basic capability can fulfill multiple requirements (a school bus could be used by a rock star).

The capability development process, for the Department of Defense (DoD), builds capabilities principally for the warfighter. Defense capabilities include airplanes, ships, tanks, weapons, personal protection for warfighters, armored vehicles, hand held radios, radar, antenna systems, intelligence gathering systems and a host of other important equipment used by the warfighter. It is a complicated and difficult to understand process . . . even for those professionals who are involved in the process each day. The process begins with the requirements process and moves to the "we don't need this stuff anymore . . . get rid of it" phase through design and production steps. All of these steps require money . . . so the DoD needs to keep Congress in the loop since Congress, by law, is the bill payer for the entire federal government capability development process.

In order to make this as simple as possible, let me use an example. At some point in time, the U.S. Army became aware of the requirement to have a tank. I know; it was awhile back. The requirement may have come from the fact that another country already had a tank. Or someone who understood the battlefield had the idea of a tank . . . something that could partially protect the warfighter at the same time as delivering heavier fire power. I don't know the story of the tank . . . I just know that, a long time ago, the military decided that it needed one.

The mission need or capability gap (something we need, but don't have) of the tank developed into a requirements document (maybe it didn't back then, but it would now). The requirements document would include how fast the tank had to move over different terrains; and the need to fire large sized cannon at some accuracy over some distance. It had to protect its occupants (the soldiers) from some size munitions. It needed to use fuel at some rate, which would allow refueling as little as possible and it need to be moved from place to place as conflicts dictated (logistics considerations). Anyway, there were some initial requirements put down which then led to an estimate of cost and a budget request given to congress.

When congress passed the defense budget, with their approval to design the tank, then, and only then, Army military and civilian scientists and engineers were given the go-ahead to start the design process for the Army tank. Thus began a process lasting many years to include concept development, prototypes, more development, testing, field testing and finally production. Every year, the Army either needed to develop or confirm the budget for the tank for the next five years. And every year there would be hiccups in the development process that would either push the tank further away from the specified delivery date or cost more money . . . sometimes both.

But the capability process did not end with the first tank designed. There have been major modifications to the original tank. It can now move faster over more terrains, shoot straighter, is more reliable and provides better protection for the warfighters within.

Another capability, maybe more familiar, is the military Jeep. It was a common piece of equipment for personnel conveyance during World War II. As requirements changed, along with the need to have one vehicle replace many different vehicles, the High Mobility Multipurpose Wheeled Vehicle, better known as the HUMVEE was developed. The HUMVEE replaced a bunch of other vehicles, including the ambulance and other trucks. Thus, one capability was able to perform multiple duties, with a better protection factor for the warfighter. Then the conflicts changed, adding more mine fields and improvised explosive devices (IEDs). This added requirements for more and better protection for our family members in conflicts. This requirement led to the Mine-Resistant Ambush Proof (MRAP) vehicle, which is currently being used. All of these capabilities improved the survival of those heroes and superheroes who are actively engaged in our conflicts.

These kinds of examples provide a rather simple way of explaining a very complicated, time sensitive, budget sensitive process. In wartime, the process may go quicker. In peace time, it seems, to those of us who have lived the process, to take forever. I have known scientists and engineers who have spent their entire careers working to deliver one capability.

There is a basic philosophy surrounding all capability development. That philosophy is to design a capability that is useful to our troops when it is finally delivered. I know . . . that is only common sense. But let's look at some highways that have been built throughout the years. The designers and futurists had to know that the I-95 corridor, along the east coast, was going to need more than a four lane (two lanes on each side) highway to carry future traffic. I'm quite certain there were monetary constraints, but, by the time that I-95 was completed, there was already a need for a bigger I-95. So . . . continuously . . . for the past decades, there has been construction on I-95 to make it bigger and wider. This has come to some consternation for the many drivers along I-95, especially during the summer months when construction is at its peak and the kids are off from school.

When a capability for a future tank, or plane or ship is considered, it is considered for the future. There may be a current need for something . . . and that capability gap is filled as soon as possible . . . but the big tax-dollar tickets are for the future. For example, if we, as a country, do not want our fathers, mothers, brothers, sisters, sons or daughters walking into battle, then we will invest in larger weapon carrying aircraft or ships with guns and missile capabilities that are more accurate from afar; or maybe drones that can collect intelligence or fire weapons from soldiers who are not at the front of the battle.

We plan for the future. We, as a nation, work to develop capabilities that can stop a conflict with minimal damage to the battlefield and to the warfighter. We improve as we go; however, our eyes are always to the future as to what capabilities we will need to have an edge on our adversary.

Also, as we try to gain an edge on some future conflict, we have learned that all friendly forces involved should be able to access the capabilities of any other friendly force. So . . . communications on the battlefield are essential and need to be copied and understood by all of our armed services and those of our allies. Integration of capabilities has become a big thing. Systems need to speak with each other. Tanks and ships and aircraft need to be in sync with the happenings of any conflict. Instead of making capability delivery easier, this has made it even more difficult . . . but necessary. The need to reduce the risk of friendly fire and confusion on the battlefield are essential.

As our requirements for future capabilities become more integrated, they become bigger and more costly. However, there is some cost advantages to having systems developed that can be used by all services and allies. The logistical costs are less. Logistics would include equipment maintenance, training, manuals, replacement parts, fuel and methods of conveyance. Logistics costs are the largest costs of any capability developed. Though logistics costs are reduced for integrated systems, the upfront costs of developing something for everyone is often higher.

As we move from hard capabilities (tanks, planes and ships) to softer capabilities (intelligence gathering, communications and command and control), the lead time for any capability to meet a future requirement diminishes. We cannot take the decade that it takes to develop a new aircraft when we are developing a communications device. For those who upgrade their cell phones every two years, you will understand why. Industry is constantly coming up with improvements to communicate more quickly and easily. For those who may understand Moore's Law, computer processing speeds were once projected to double every two years. Processing speeds are probably doubling every year and things are heating up even faster as we move forward.

Computer processing speeds have driven the once primitive cell phone to capabilities never before possible. There are now more ways to communicate, using a cell phone or tablet, than simply making a call. The need to use devices similar to cell phones, and less like walkie-talkies, or large hand held and back carried devices, is driving the current capability process for communications.

Also, when our country and its allies are talking to each other, and our equipment is integrated and "talking" to each other, we do not want those, with whom we are in conflict, hearing what we are saying. And, at the same time, it would be good to know what those with whom we are in conflict are saying. It gives us an advantage. It gives us an edge. It is an advantage that the other side is working on also. The battlefield has always been a place where those in conflict are constantly trying to gain an edge.

Weapons provide one edge. It is why we develop larger and more lethal weapons. We not only want an edge; but we want the other side to think twice before they enter into a conflict. We try not to use weapons of mass destruction. They are there mostly to be used as a warning against starting a fight. They are a deterrent against future conflict.

Intelligence provides another edge. As long as wars have been fought, intelligence gathering has been a part. Before aircraft had guns, they were used, with photographers hanging over the sides, to gain intelligence. As new ways of communicating are developed, new ways of gaining an advantage over those new ways are necessary to gain an edge and to avert a new conflict.

So . . . the capabilities development process for intelligence gathering has to be a quicker process (technology is changing rapidly) and cover a wider base of communications (there are more ways now to communicate and will be even more ways in the future). Though some may disagree, I believe it is essential that an intelligence system be designed so that as many future communications tools as possible can be intercepted. I believe it especially essential now that those, who may be planning some future adversarial event, currently live and work on our shores. And they appear no different than we. And we, as a nation, would be appalled with the idea of treating anyone, on our shores, as different.

WEAPONS OF MASS DESTRUCTION

Prior to September 11, 2001, few would have thought of a commercial aircraft as a weapon of mass destruction. But our enemies did. They could see the value in using our own commercial aircraft, full of fuel, as a weapon to destroy thousands of lives and billions of dollars in property. But why couldn't we see that purpose? And how come commercial aircraft have not been used previously by pilots to kill our own citizens?

I believe the answer to why we do not kill our own stems from my previous discussion of heroes. The vast majority of the employees in our commercial airline industry are heroes. They come to work every day to do their job and provide for their families. Pilots, flight attendants, air-traffic controllers, mechanics, baggage handlers, security and employees of any other important aspect of the commercial airline and airport industry are solid citizens of this country, who work to provide for themselves, their families and their customers. Those, who are late in arriving to their destination, or who find their luggage lost, may differ in their opinions of the industry; however, I believe the record of the industry is a rather safe one. Accidents happen, and when they do they are horrific; however, they are accidents. They are not planned destruction of human life and property. Though the capability of using aircraft to kill has been demonstrated, it is not a capability that is used.

There are processes in place to assure those who travel the airways that they will be safe and will eventually arrive at their destination unharmed. There are massive training requirements for pilots . . . hours and hours of training in order to safely and intelligently move from point A to point B. There are also massive training requirements for flight attendants and security personnel and the other jobs behind the scenes. These training requirements never stop. Those in the industry are constantly reminded of the skills and knowledge required to move people around the country and the world.

There are many other processes in place to insure safety . . . maximum hours of work for the pilots . . . minimum distances between aircraft in flight. It is neither my intent nor my ability to list all of the processes in place to assure safety in flight. It is only my intent to relay that there are many rules and processes in place to insure safety. Add to those rules and processes, the dedicated workforce, who adhere to those rules and processes, and we have maintained a mostly friendly sky.

. . .

So . . . how about weapons of mass destruction that were designed to be weapons of mass destruction?

Nuclear weapons are considered to be weapons of mass destruction and are also considered to be a deterrent weapon system. Nuclear weapons are located and stored on our land and on the land of our friends and foes. I have faith that we will only use them if they are used on us; however, what stops someone from launching one out of mischief or hate?

I go back again to my beginning discussion about heroes. The men and women who work in the nuclear defense program are dedicated personnel. There is a mixture of military and civilian employees, who come to work every day to support themselves and their families. They take their jobs seriously. They are also highly trained and adhere to strenuous personnel reliability requirements.

I never worked in the nuclear defense program, but I did work in the chemical agent defense program. I worked twenty years with seasoned professionals who performed the role of protectors of chemical agent weapons of mass destruction seriously. As a manager of some of the laboratories, where chemical agent research took place, I was required to be in the chemical personnel reliability program. It was a rigorous program of clearances and close supervision. No one worked with chemical agent alone. There was always a buddy with you. That buddy provided a safety net and contributed to the security of the materials being used.

Though most of the stockpile of chemical agents, once stored on these shores, has been destroyed, there is still a need for chemical agent research. We need to know what is happening around the world in relation to new chemical agents. We need to know how to decontaminate those chemicals. We need to know how to detect those chemicals when we come upon them. We need to know how to protect our troops who may, sometime in the future, come upon them. We need an edge always when it comes to new ways to harm our citizenry. We prepare for that edge through research of new capabilities and ways to better defend against existing capabilities from those who wish us harm.

So . . . whether it is nuclear, chemical or biological, there are many dedicated public servants who work with and protect others from these scary weapons. We are in fear of these weapons because of the damage they can do to life as we know it. We are in fear of them because of the way they are portrayed in movies and television. It is not my intent to convince anyone that we need these weapons of mass destruction for a deterrent; or that we need them to conduct research. My intent is to say that we have them; and that we require a dedicated and trusted resource to manage them . . . and protect our citizens and our friends from them.

SYSTEMS OF MASS INTELLIGENCE

Now that I have addressed weapons of mass destruction, let me discuss systems of mass intelligence. I do not see intelligence as a weapon; though the gathering of intelligence and the subsequent identification of an adversary could be used as a method of gaining access to that adversary and lead to their capture and demise. I see that as similar to the duty of a sniper. I do not see that as mass destruction.

I have already discussed capability development briefly. The need for methods and processes to capture data and communications flowing around the globe has gotten more complicated with newer, quicker and more reliable methods to communicate. Sixty years ago, we had a pretty good idea of both who and where our adversaries were. Communications were mostly over wire and using radio signals. It was a simpler world in which to gain intelligence. There was no internet. There were few satellites used for communications. There were no personal computers. There were no hand held computers. For those who can remember, my parents had a party phone line. There was at least one other household that could listen in on our conversations whenever we accessed our home phone. Those are probably considered the "good old days" by some.

As communications and data sharing have exploded, the capabilities needed to gather some of the data shared by our adversaries, by necessity, have increased substantially. We need to be faster and broader in our communications/data/signals gathering in order to determine if our adversaries are planning something. We need to know how fast and where we need to react. As I stated previously, we used to know where our adversaries were. Now we do not. They can be residing, peacefully at the moment, on our land. They can be planning anywhere. They can be fully capable of destroying life and property anywhere in our country or on an ally's soil. If we are to defend our country, then we need to know what our adversaries are planning. We can use spies to infiltrate their planning cells or we can listen in on their conversations and data exchanges or we can do both. The smaller the planning cell, the harder it is to infiltrate. And, the smaller the planning cell, the harder it is to gain intelligence. That is where intelligence gathering becomes both a science and an art.

I would have to say to those who are truly offended by the government's ability to access signals and data that most of us really have nothing interesting to say. I'm sorry if I offend. I would also add that if some of us are doing something really stupid, and we don't want others to know about it, the probability is greater than zero that what we are doing will be on some social media site or someone will take a picture, on their phone, of our antics. The government cares not about our affairs or misdoings. However, if we are breaking the law, well . . . other law enforcement agencies may be interested and they have their own methods of capture.

The National Security Agency (NSA) is about foreign intelligence. Other intelligence agencies and law enforcement agencies handle the intelligence within the borders of our country. I know NSA is about foreign intelligence because I had to swear to uphold its laws and I had to read those laws and document that I read those laws at least annually. Those, who work at NSA, know the laws and rules by which it operates regardless of the capabilities residing within its confines. It is one thing to know the extent of the capabilities to gain access into communications and data flows. It is quite another to use those capabilities in an unlawful way. There are processes and checks and double checks to assure the laws are followed. Like those who guard our weapons systems, even those weapons of mass destruction, it is the everyday heroes who keep our defense systems and intelligence gathering systems able and lawful.

. . .

Before I leave the subject of mass intelligence, let me also explain, in plain numbers, what it might take to listen in on every phone conversation taking place and read every e-mail being written each and every day.

Let's assume that out of the approximately three-hundred million people, living in our country, that maybe only one-hundred million people actually use communications devices each day. That would eliminate those under maybe twelve (a conservative age) who do not have cell phones or tablets or other devices with which they can gain access to from some Wi-Fi network or satellite. I would also eliminate those who may be too old to care about the cooler technologies . . . those who have to go to their kids for their assistance . . . though they still would use some phone device. I know it's a conservative number. There are probably more than one-hundred million who converse each day using some device . . . other than face to face.

So . . . if the government were trying to listen to one-hundred million people conversing, texting, face-timing, e-mailing, then the government would have to hire about one-hundred million people to do so. Assuming those the government hires would only work one shift, then the government would probably need about two-hundred million people in order to listen to and watch those one hundred million during their waking hours (assuming the hundred-million the government is trying to listen to sleep for eight hours). But, you say, we don't need that many people because we can just collect all of the communications signals and data and look at them at a later date. Well – what would be the point? If the government truly wants to discover what the adversary is planning, they don't want to look at that information after something bad has happened.

The government did not design a capability to listen to everyone in the country all of the time. The government designed a capability to target our adversaries to discover their next target.

You might be thinking that I am talking down to my reader . . . that you are smart enough to know that the government can't and won't hire two-hundred million people to listen and maintain surveillance on another one-hundred million. I know you know that . . . but I feel a need to exaggerate a little . . . because that is what is going on in the media. We, as a public, are being led to believe that the NSA can and does listen to everyone pretty much all of the time. That is a mathematic improbability. The drama makes no logical sense to me.

Then who are the small and limited number of analysts, at the NSA, listening to? I don't know. In probabilistic terms, if you are a citizen, and you are not communicating with one of our adversaries, then your only concern is social media. The probability of anyone, in the government, caring about what you have to say is zero. If you are an adversary, or you are conversing, by any means, with one of our adversaries, then the probability of someone, in the government, listening, is greater than zero.

The people, who go to work every day at the NSA are solid citizens. They love their family. They love their country. They are heroes to me. They work to protect this country. Though they have massive capability at their fingertips, they point that capability where it does the most good for our country . . . not where it will do harm . . . not to where the media would pretend.

CHANGING THE WAY A NATION THINKS OR ACTS

My original title for this chapter was "changing the way a nation thinks". But the more I thought about that the more I doubted whether anyone can really change the way people think . . . not quickly anyway. That process takes many years and generations. However, we can change the laws of a nation to coerce its citizens to act a certain way, even if they do not agree. So . . . we can change the way some citizens think and we can certainly change the way the nation is expected to act.

As I began to put this treatise together, I couldn't get past the idea that others, in our past, have fought hard to change the way we think or act without a traitorous act. I am quite certain that those who do betray this country do so with some noble thought in their minds. If they sell secrets to other nation states for money . . . so that they can have nicer things, well I have trouble seeing anything noble. However, if they believe they can change the course of history by enabling an adversary or by highlighting to the public something they consider unfair, then maybe they feel there is something noble in their own minds concerning their actions.

So . . . who might I list as some others, who have performed noble acts of conscience without betraying their country? Well . . . this is supposed to be a short treatise. Volumes have been written about those who have faced adversity in trying to change the way a nation thinks.

I'll use two rather quick examples. There are many, many others in this nation and in other nations . . . people who have changed the way their nation thought, or at least acted . . . and who have changed the way much of the world has thought. The two examples, for me, for this nation, are Abraham Lincoln and Dr. Martin Luther King. I am not going to go into the history of these individuals. There are many books about Abraham Lincoln and Dr. Martin Luther King. Those books would be a much better way to gain insight into their lives. I would prefer, here, to simply discuss two alternate ways to get a point across to those who surround you.

The first way to change the way a nation thinks or acts is to run for political office. That is the method used by Abraham Lincoln. He believed in something. He was passionate about something. So he got his law degree and started running for offices . . . local offices at first . . . then the national scene. He was harassed and ridiculed; he lost his bid for office a few times; but he stayed his course. He became the President of the United States. He influenced a change in the course of our history.

Another way to change the way a nation thinks or acts is to become an activist. An activist rallies the cause. An activist leads the fight for what they believe is right. Dr. Martin Luther King was an activist . . . a very good activist. Dr. Martin Luther King rallied the forces for a noble cause that has changed the course of our history. He was harassed and ridiculed. There were forces at work that would have had him fail . . . that wanted him to fail. Like Abraham Lincoln, he stayed the course. Like Abraham Lincoln, he paid the price of noble leadership and change with his life.

Though many, who change the course of history, are not assassinated, they do devote their lives to their passion . . . to the changes they wish to occur. They are not thieves. They are not liars. They are not traitors. Nor are they perfect. None of us are. But their nobility is true. They want what they believe is best for all . . . and they are willing to give up their lives for the cause.

Those, who would change the way a nation thinks or acts, do not run away from the fight. They do not flee to another country for protection. They do not use someone else to fight for them. They are not playing the part of Robin Hood . . . they do not steal from the rich to give to the poor. They use their own force of personality, in their own nation, to bring about change.

Though others may disagree with them; though they may be harassed; though they may be ridiculed, they stay the course. They rally the cause. They convince the citizenry. They move politicians to change the laws of the land. They do not run away.

EPILOGUE

I do not know how many lives will be lost due to some of our intelligence gathering capabilities being given away. I do know that more tax dollars will be spent to fix the damage . . . not less. When our adversaries recognized our personnel carrier weaknesses and decided to blow up our HUMVEES, with our troops inside, we had to quickly design and field the MRAP. When an adversary knows our advantage and gains an edge, it is our troops and our taxpayers who pay the price to gain that edge back.

I have attempted, in this treatise, to answer the five questions stated previously from my own experience . . . as a citizen of this nation and as a devoted employee of the Defense Department and of the Office of the Director of National Intelligence. In answering my own questions, I have attempted to begin a larger conversation . . . not necessarily about the legitimacy of what our government does in relation to offensive and defensive capabilities; but why it does what it does, along with who uses those capabilities and how they are used.

I have attempted to remove some of the drama our own media, in doing its job, imparts to the conversation. Knowing some of the facts may help the conversation to return to the defense of this nation . . . and away from the spying on its citizens.

Most of all, I wanted to begin a conversation concerning the expected behaviors of this nation's citizenry. What is it we want the defenders of this nation to do? Will we honor those who divulge our offensive and defensive capabilities to our adversaries? Do we no longer agree with the old adage that "loose lips sink ships"? Do we no longer value all of the men and women who go to work each day to protect and defend us . . . so that we can write and read and speak what we wish?

Do we no longer value an oath?